CURRENT
SCIENCE®

Bugs on Your Body

Nature's Creepiest Creatures Live on You!

By John Perritano

Reading Adviser: Cecilia Minden-Cupp, Ph.D., Literacy Consultant
Science Curriculum Content Consultant: Debra Voege, M.A.

 Gareth Stevens
Publishing

Please visit our web site at **www.garethstevens.com**.
For a free color catalog describing Gareth Stevens Publishing's list of
high-quality books, call 1-800-542-2595 (USA) or 1-800-387-3178 (Canada).
Gareth Stevens Publishing's fax: 1-877-542-2596

Library of Congress Cataloging-in-Publication Data

Perritano, John.
    Bugs on your body : nature's creepiest creatures live on you! / by John Perritano;
reading consultant, Cecilia Minden-Cupp ; science curriculum
content consultant, Debra Voege.
      p. cm. — (Current science)
    Includes bibliographical references and index.
    ISBN-10: 1-4339-2058-1   ISBN-13: 978-1-4339-2058-5 (lib. bdg.)
    1. Parasitic insects—Juvenile literature. 2. Insects—
Juvenile literature. I. Title.
QL496.12.P469   2010
595.716'5—dc22
                                    2009006687

This edition first published in 2010 by
Gareth Stevens Publishing
A Weekly Reader® Company
1 Reader's Digest Road
Pleasantville, NY 10570-7000 USA

Copyright © 2010 by Gareth Stevens, Inc.

Current Science™ is a trademark of Weekly Reader Corporation. Used under license.

Gareth Stevens Executive Managing Editor: Lisa M. Herrington
Gareth Stevens Senior Editor: Barbara Bakowski
Gareth Stevens Cover Designer: Keith Plechaty

Created by **Q2AMedia**
Editor: Jessica Cohn
Art Director: Rahul Dhiman
Designer: Harleen Mehta
Photo Researcher: Kamal Kumar
Illustrators: Indranil Ganguly, Kusum Kala, Madhavi Poddar, Rohit Sharma

Photo credits (t = top; b = bottom; c = center; l = left; r = right):
Eye of Science/Photo Researchers, Inc: cover, Sebastian Kaulitzki/Shutterstock: title page, Darlyne A.
Murawski/Photolibrary: 4, Juanmonino/Istockphoto: 5, Hulton Archive/Stringer/Getty Images: 6, Avava/
Shutterstock: 7, Callalloo Candcy/Fotolia: 8, Warren Rosenberg/Fotolia: 9, Sonya Etchison/Fotolia: 10b,
Dan Pettersson/Istockphoto: 10cr, Dhoxax/Shutterstock: 12, Juniors Bildarchiv/Photolibrary: 13, Arlindo71/
Istockphoto: 14tl, Arlindo71/Istockphoto: 14tr, Dennis Kunkel/Photolibrary: 14c, Tracy Whiteside/Shutterstock:
15b, Darlyne A. Murawski/Photolibrary: 15cr, Moodboard/Corbis: 16, Laurent/Rilhac/Photolibrary: 17, Chno
Liotet/Photolibrary: 19t, Parker Deen/Istockphoto: 19b, Sebastian Kaulitzki/Shutterstock: 20t, Volker Steger/
Photolibrary: 20b, Darlyne A. Murawski/Photolibrary: 21, John Downer/Photolibrary: 22, Dr. Kenneth Greer/
Getty Images: 23, Edward Todd/Istockphoto: 24, Charlie Drevstam/Photolibrary: 25, Bob Sacha/Corbis:
26-27, Eye of Science/Photolibrary: 28, JLP/Jose L. Pelaez/Corbis: 29, David Scharf/Photolibrary: 30, Knorre/
Dreamstime: 31, Ed Andrieski/Associated Press: 32, Benoist Carpentier/World Health Organization: 33,
Winston Luzier/Transtock/Corbis: 34, Brett Lamb/Istockphoto: 35cr, Walter Bibikow/Corbis: 35b, Phil Date/
Shutterstock: 36, David Burder/Getty Images: 37, Arlindo71/Istockphoto: 38t, Sonya Etchison/Fotolia: 38b,
Polka Dot Images/Jupiter Images: 38-39, Sebastian Kaulitzki/Shutterstock: 39tl, Douglas Allen/Istockphoto:
39tr, Artur Tiutenko/Shutterstock: 39c, Carolina K. Smith, M.D./Shutterstock: 39bc, Sergey Doronin: 39b,
Ryosha/Shutterstock: 40, John D. McHugh/Associated Press: 41t, Reto Stöckli, Nazmi El Saleous, and Marit
Jentoft-Nilsen/NASA GSFC: 41b, Scott Harms/Istockphoto: 42, Bmpix/Istockphoto: 43t, Kim Taylor/npl/
Minden Pictures: 43b, Glen Needham: 44, Morgan Lane Photography/Shutterstock: 47
Q2A Media Art Bank: 7t, 9t, 11, 17b, 18, 23t, 25c, 27 36, 37t

Printed in the United States of America

1 2 3 4 5 6 7 8 9 12 11 10 09

CONTENTS

Words in **boldface** type are defined in the glossary.

Chapter 1

What Bugs You?

Bugs are everywhere. They feast on you while you sleep. They drink your blood! They make you itch. Some bugs hope for a chance to crawl into your ear. Others just want to burrow under your skin. Bugs like living in your bed. They love living on your dog.

Magnified view of a bedbug filled with human blood

PARASITE PESTS

There are thousands of **species**, or kinds, of bugs in the world. Some bugs, such as the ladybug, seem pleasant enough. Other bugs act like cannibals. They eat their own kind. Still others like to dine on humans and animals.

Many bugs are **parasites**. Parasites are **organisms** that live on, or in, another living organism, called a **host**. Two types of parasites exist. Some parasites, such as fleas, live *on* the body of an animal or a human. Scientists call these parasites **ectoparasites**. Other parasites, such as the tapeworm, live *inside* a person or an animal. Scientists call those bugs **endoparasites**.

Asleep or awake, everyone is a host for bugs.

A WORLD OF WORMS

Some parasites, such as fleas, are fairly easy to spot. Sometimes, though, you cannot see the bug that attacks you. More than 1.3 billion people carry hookworms, a kind of roundworm, in their small **intestines**. Most of those people do not have a clue that the worms are there. Roundworms of many kinds like to live in human and animal intestines. Another kind of roundworm infects about 1.5 billion people, making the hosts very sick.

FAST FACT
At bedtime, the female pinworm often finds her way out of a human's intestines. She lays eggs at the lower opening. The eggs end up on pajamas or bedsheets.

5

Fleas spread the Black Death, which killed millions of people in the Middle Ages.

SPREADING DISEASES

All people are victims of parasitic bugs at one time or another. Many parasites, such as ticks, are very common. Others, such as the human botfly, are rare. Some parasitic bugs are fairly harmless. Others sicken and even kill humans and animals. The bigger bugs can carry smaller bugs, called **microbes**. Microbes can cause disease.

PLAGUED BY PESTS

Disease-carrying insects have been around a long, long time. For instance, one of the most feared diseases carried by insects is the **bubonic plague**. The plague was responsible for the deaths of millions of Europeans in the Middle Ages. The same illness killed millions more throughout history.

Fleas transmit the **bacterium** that causes the plague. During the Middle Ages, rats often inhabited homes and businesses. Those rats carried fleas. If an infected flea bit someone, that person usually died within a week.

The plague is still around, although outbreaks are rare. Wild rodents carry the diseased fleas. In the United States, the plague infects 10 to 15 people a year. Today, doctors can treat the disease with a powerful group of drugs called **antibiotics**.

Antibiotics fight disease-causing bacteria carried by bugs.

When bubonic plague hit Europe in the Middle Ages, people called it the Black Death. At least 25 million people died. As dead bodies piled up, fear overtook the continent.

Sicily, an Italian island, was one of the first parts of Europe to feel the sting of the disease. By January 1348, the Italian ports of Genoa and Venice began seeing their first cases of the plague.

Officials in Venice tried to stop the disease from spreading. They ordered ships from plague-affected areas to anchor offshore for 40 days. In Latin, this order was written as *quaranta giorni*. Today, the English word *quarantine* means to isolate a person with a catching disease.

Chapter 2

Friendly
Fleas
AND TICKS

Scratch . . . scratch . . . scratch! What is wrong with Whiskers? Chances are, the cat has fleas or ticks. Wherever there are animals that can serve as hosts, fleas and ticks are happy guests.

FLEA-BITTEN

About 250 species of fleas live in North America. Some fleas move from host to host. Other fleas like to stay in one place. Fleas burrow into an animal's skin. The animal can become sick if a female flea dies inside the skin.

Fleas are flat and reddish brown. These pests have an **exoskeleton** but no wings. Fleas are tiny—just 1/16 to 1/8 of an inch (2 to 3 millimeters) long. These pests have sharp **mandibles**, or jaws. The bugs drink blood through a **proboscis**, which works like a straw. Fleas dine on the **feces** of other fleas. They also like to chow down on dry skin and on smaller bugs, such as mites.

What if the insect world gave gold medals? The flea would take home the gold in the high jump. Fleas can jump 200 times their own height. How high is that? That is roughly 14 to 16 inches (36 to 41 centimeters) high.

Humans cannot jump as high, in comparison. A 6-foot-tall (2-meter-tall) person would have to be able to leap over the Empire State Building in New York City to beat a flea! The world high-jump record for humans is 8.03 feet (2.45 meters).

A microscope with a special light helps you see inside a flea's body.

TICK TALK

In backyards, forests, and gardens lurks a bug with blood on its mind. Dog blood! Deer blood! Human blood! Any kind of blood! Ticks perch on plants, such as tall grass. As unsuspecting **prey** brush by, the ticks crawl onto their victims and feed on their blood.

Unlike fleas, ticks are not insects. Ticks are **arachnids**. Spiders and scorpions are arachnids, too. Arachnids have four pairs of legs and no **antennae**.

Many species of ticks live in different areas of the world. The American dog tick, for instance, is native to North America. The **nymph** and **larva** forms of this species feed on small animals such as mice. The adult dog tick feeds on larger **mammals**, including dogs and even humans! The brown dog tick, however, rarely bothers people. That tick prefers to get its blood meal from a four-legged Fido.

A tick senses body heat to locate a victim.

Fleas and ticks can make the move from your pet to you.

YOU DO IT!

Make a Bug Catcher

What You Need

- clear glass jar, such as a mayonnaise jar
- twigs and grass
- sugar or candy

What You Do

Step 1

Remove all labels from the jar. Wash the jar with soap and water. Rinse and dry. Place some twigs and grass inside the jar. Add the sugar or candy.

Step 2

Take the jar outdoors. Place it in a grassy area. Look for a small stick to lean against the jar as a ramp.

Step 3

After an hour or two, see what bugs you have caught.

What Happened?

The bugs were attracted to the sweet scent of the sugar and marched into the jar.

BAD BUGS

Fleas and ticks carry a variety of diseases. Over 30 species of fleas can pass along illnesses. One of those illnesses is a form of typhus. It can affect the brain, heart, and kidneys. Flea-borne diseases can lead to other sicknesses, too. Fleas carry bubonic plague, which can turn into **pneumonic plague**. This lung disease spreads easily through coughs and sneezes.

Wood ticks and other ticks spread Rocky Mountain spotted fever—and not just in the Rockies. Symptoms include a rash and stomachaches. Deer ticks and black-legged ticks spread Lyme disease. The disease resembles the flu at first. Symptoms include tiredness and muscle aches. A circular rash may appear. Doctors treat both diseases with antibiotics. See a doctor if you are bitten by a flea or a tick and get sick.

Ticks that live on deer can transmit diseases to people.

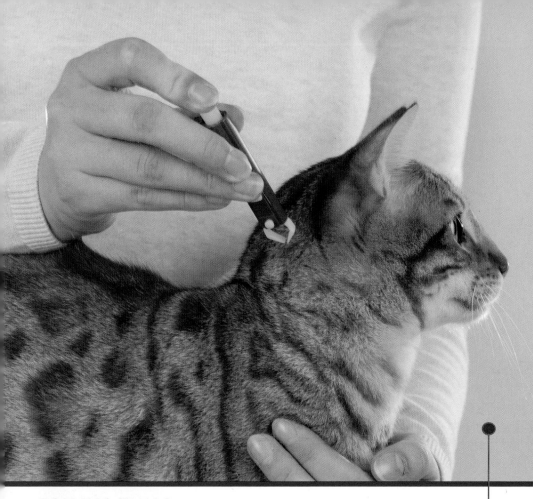

Ick! A tick! Flea and tick protection is important for pets.

FOILING FLEAS AND TICKS

Fleas and ticks have lived on Earth for millions of years. We cannot kill all of them, but we can protect ourselves. Special shampoos, collars, and medicines help control fleas and ticks on pets. **Exterminators** can kill bugs by spraying **pesticides** that are safe for the environment.

You can take precautions when hiking, gardening, or playing outdoors. Wear long pants, long-sleeve shirts, and high socks to keep ticks off your skin. Have an adult spray your skin with bug **repellent**.

WHAT DO YOU THINK?

What might be some other ways to stay protected against fleas and ticks?

Chapter 3

FEELING LOUSY

Each fall, schools everywhere go buggy! For some students, a new school year brings a nasty surprise: head lice! These tiny pests are the most common human parasites in the United States.

THE LOWDOWN ON LICE

Head lice are insects that live and lay eggs in human hair. They do not transmit diseases, but they can cause a very itchy scalp.

Head lice do not attack dirty people in particular. These bugs attack anyone they can. Some schools have **infestations**. Lice spread quickly through head-to-head contact among classmates.

WHAT A LOUSE!

Head lice live close to the scalp to keep warm. Their six legs have claws to hold on to hair strands. A louse's favorite hangouts are near the neck, behind the ears, and near the top of the head. This flat, gray, wingless creature is about one-tenth of an inch (2 mm) long. That is about the size of a sesame seed.

FAST FACT
Head lice become darker as they grow.

The head louse looks like a shiny dot on a piece of hair.

Head lice like to hide near the scalp.

WHAT'S FOR DINNER?

Head lice dine on small amounts of blood a few times a day. They use a long straw-like tube, called a **stylet**, to draw blood from their victims. These bugs cannot live more than a day away from a human host. Head lice dine mostly on children between the ages of 3 and 11.

Lice crawl. They cannot fly or jump. Children get head lice by sharing clothing, such as scarves and hats. Lice can also spread when kids share brushes or headphones. The bugs rub off onto things, such as towels and sheets.

CONTROLLING HEAD LICE

Have you ever heard someone say, "Prevention is the best cure"? You can do several things to keep lice from making a home on you. Don't share items such as combs, hats, and clothes. Wash towels, sheets, and bedspreads in hot water.

What if the critters camp out on your scalp? Doctors recommend using a special mix of chemicals to kill the lice. You should also comb through hair carefully to remove any eggs.

Special products can kill head lice.

A Hair-Raising Job

Dee Wright is a killer. She has head lice in her crosshairs. Wright is the founder of Hairforce: Lice Assassins.

Hairforce is a spa in London, England. In the spa, Wright and her coworkers remove head lice from the scalps of children. First, the Lice Assassins vacuum a child's head. Next, they use a lice comb to clear out the tiny lice eggs, called nits. Using special tweezers, the nitpickers grab hold of each louse and remove it. See you later, lice!

IT'S A LOUSE'S LIFE !

Lice go through three stages in which they change form completely. The life cycle from egg to adult takes about a month.

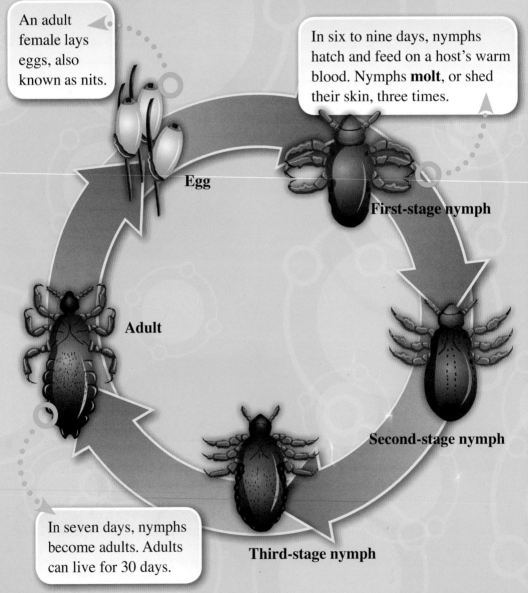

An adult female lays eggs, also known as nits.

In six to nine days, nymphs hatch and feed on a host's warm blood. Nymphs **molt**, or shed their skin, three times.

Egg

First-stage nymph

Adult

Second-stage nymph

Third-stage nymph

In seven days, nymphs become adults. Adults can live for 30 days.

The tiny *Demodex* mite can be seen only with the help of a microscope.

PRETTY HAIRY

Head lice have plenty of company. Some *Demodex* mites like to live in human hair, too. These mites live near hair **follicles**. A follicle is a narrow tube that leads from the surface of the skin to the hair root. The mites also live in skin openings called **pores**.

Like ticks, mites are arachnids, not insects. Two known species of *Demodex* mites live on humans. These mites usually live near the scalp, eyebrows, and eyelashes. They are sometimes called "eyelash mites." The mini-mites like living in the skin of the cheeks and nose, too. They can spread from host to host but are mostly harmless.

The *Demodex* mite likes living in eyebrows and eyelashes.

Chapter 4

Bedtime SNACK ATTACK!

When you go to bed, you might not be sleeping alone. Tiny creatures might be crawling on you! These hungry creatures want to feast on blood. They are not the vampires of horror stories. They are much more real! Meet the tiny monsters known as bedbugs.

Bedbugs cause itching but do not spread diseases.

CREATURES OF THE NIGHT

Bedbugs are reddish brown. An adult bedbug is about 0.2 inch (5 mm) long. When a person sleeps, the bugs go to work! They pierce the skin of their prey with long beaks. Although they do not carry disease, bedbugs make their victims itch and scratch.

The bugs can hide in any seam or furniture crack. Their ability to hide makes finding and killing them difficult! Female bedbugs lay eggs on mattresses, in box springs, and in cracks in floorboards. The eggs hatch into nymphs. Newly hatched nymphs need to feed immediately. The bugs are nymphs for 32 to 48 days. Then they shed their skin several times before becoming adults. Bedbugs mate as soon as they become adults.

FAST FACT
Is there a crack in your floor wide enough to fit a playing card? That crack is big enough to hide a bedbug.

Pest control experts have a new way to kill bedbugs: by baking them! Exterminators raise the room temperature with a special machine.

BEDBUGS IN THE NEWS

Bedbug infestation is on the rise. Many people think bedbugs live only in run-down buildings. However, the pests are popping up even in fancy hotel rooms. The bugs are also overrunning some college dormitories.

Why is this happening? Experts say bedbugs have been stowing away in luggage, purses, and other carried items. Travelers visit countries where bedbugs thrive. The travelers then bring the bugs home with them.

Bedbugs are more than happy to take over their new space.

Changes in pesticide use have also made life easier for the bugs. Bedbugs have started resisting some chemicals. Other chemicals strong enough to kill them have been outlawed. Those chemicals are no longer used because they made animals and people sick.

FEELING THE BITE

Bedbugs are becoming a problem around the globe. The bedbug problem in Sydney, Australia, is bad. At Westmead Hospital in that city, officials teach people how to detect and control the bloodsuckers. Between 2000 and 2006, Westmead had a 4,500 percent increase in calls from people wondering what to do about bedbugs!

Bedbugs are a nuisance in the United States, too. In December 2008, about 140 landlords in Minneapolis, Minnesota, attended the first meeting of a bedbug task force. All but five said they had problems with bedbugs on their properties.

Dog Detectives

Bella is a dog with a nose for bedbugs. Most Labrador retrievers would rather romp around a yard or chase a ball. Bella loves to find bedbugs. Bella and her handler, Greg Broberg, travel the country, sniffing out the creatures.

Broberg trained Bella to pick up the scent of bedbugs and their eggs. Bella is not the only pooch with a nose for bugs. In New Haven, Connecticut, an apartment complex recently had trained beagles look for bedbugs before the bugs had a chance to spread.

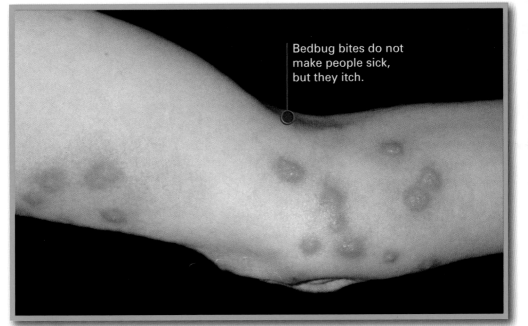

Bedbug bites do not make people sick, but they itch.

THE BUGS STOP HERE!

Getting rid of bedbugs can be difficult. They live in dry, dark places. These pests do not usually come out during the day. Bedbugs hide in mattresses, behind pictures on walls, and even between the pages of books!

If your house is infested, you might need to hire a professional exterminator. Exterminators spray pesticides throughout the rooms. An exterminator might also have to treat apartments that are next to affected apartments.

Exterminators are trained to battle bedbugs and other pests.

Bedbugs do not usually travel far from people, their source of food. If you are waking up with bites, a doctor can help figure out if you need help.

What can people do to keep bedbugs away? Inspect luggage and other travel items. Do not take and reuse mattresses or other household items from the trash. Vacuum near and on the bed. Clean linens regularly.

Bedbugs sometimes spread when people sleep on used mattresses.

MEET THE DUST MITE

Having trouble with dust mites? Dust mites are eyeless arachnids with eight hairy legs. Their heads, which have no antennae, are rough and tough. These creatures are tiny, but they can cause big problems.

Dust mites are round. Their color is often creamy white. They also have a striped **cuticle**. That is the tough outer layer of the organism.

North American dust mites are so small that you need a microscope or a magnifying glass to see them. They live in bedding, carpets, and elsewhere. Mites like places that are warm and humid. Dust mites die in cool, dry air.

When magnified, dust mites look scary. It's their droppings, though, that make trouble.

Adult female dust mites lay about 80 eggs. A six-legged larva hatches from each egg. When the larva molts, an eight-legged nymph emerges. Later, the nymph becomes an adult. The entire process, from egg to adult, takes about a month. Adult dust mites generally live one to three months.

WHAT DO YOU THINK?
What if people could wipe out bugs? What would happen to bats, birds, and other animals that eat insects?

LIFE CYCLE OF A MITE

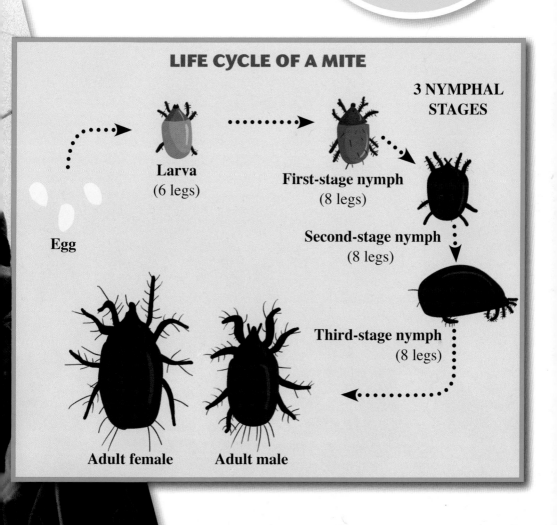

Egg

Larva
(6 legs)

First-stage nymph
(8 legs)

3 NYMPHAL STAGES

Second-stage nymph
(8 legs)

Third-stage nymph
(8 legs)

Adult female   Adult male

ATTACK OF THE DUST MITES

Guess who is coming to dinner? From 100,000 to 10 million dust mites probably share your bed. What is on the menu? You!

Dust mites feast on dead skin. Humans shed about one-fifth of an ounce (7 grams) of dead skin each week. Dead skin is also known as **dander**. The dander of people and animals makes up about 80 percent of the dust you can see floating in a sunlit room. Thousands of mites can live in the skin you shed in one day!

Dust mites look like specks—until you see them magnified by a microscope.

ACHOO!

Each mite makes about 20 particles of waste droppings each day. The droppings become airborne when they mix with household dust. Many people have an **allergy** to dust mite droppings. Breathing in the dust can cause wheezing, sneezing, watery eyes, and a runny nose. In some people, dust mites trigger **asthma**. Asthma is a disease of the lungs.

FAST FACT
A study at a university in London, England, found that if you do not make your bed in the morning, the number of dust mites will go down. Why? An unmade bed allows sheets to dry out. Bedbugs like damp places.

Dust mites make people with allergies sneeze.

Chapter 5

Hungry for BLOOD

As the Sun sets on a warm summer day, flying insects dance overhead. At night, they flit in the glare of a streetlight. These hip-hopping insects are mosquitoes.

A microscope makes the mosquito look hundreds of times bigger than its actual size.

Only female mosquitoes bite us! They need blood to make eggs.

BUZZ OFF

Mosquitoes are bloodsuckers. For 30 million years, these pesky creatures have been buzzing around the planet. Approximately 2,700 species of mosquitoes exist. About 150 species live in North America.

Mosquito is the Spanish word for "little fly." Unlike most flies, however, mosquitoes bite humans and animals. Specifically, female mosquitoes bite. The males feed only on plants.

Like all insects, mosquitoes have three main body sections. They are the head, the **thorax**, and the **abdomen**. The head consists of eyes and a brain. Females have a proboscis, a hollow tube used to draw blood from prey. Mosquitoes have two wings and six legs. They live near standing water, where they breed. The water could be anything from a puddle to a pond to rainwater in a wheelbarrow.

FAST FACT
Mosquitoes can beat their wings 300 to 500 times a second.

DEATH BY MOSQUITO

The mosquito is a master at spreading diseases. When mosquitoes drink blood, they can transmit disease-causing microbes. Malaria, West Nile fever, and yellow fever are just some of the illnesses that the mosquitoes carry.

Malaria is a major health issue in some places. Worldwide, 300 million to 500 million people get malaria each year. The disease is a problem mostly in Africa, Asia, eastern Europe, and the South Pacific.

West Nile virus is becoming a problem in the United States. According to the Centers for Disease Control and Prevention, more than 1,300 people in the United States became sick with West Nile virus in 2008. Forty-four of those people died.

FATAL ATTRACTION

Why are people such attractive prey? Mosquitoes are very good at detecting the carbon dioxide that people breathe out. Mosquitoes are also attracted to body heat. The insects can even spot people's bright-colored clothing. Mosquitoes have **compound eyes**. Their eyes are very good at seeing bright colors, such as red and yellow. When a mosquito sees a flash of color, the bug flies closer, hoping to find a source of blood!

Always have an adult apply insect repellent.

Nets: Covering a Continent

Mosquitoes infect millions of people each year with a variety of diseases, from malaria to yellow fever. Mosquito nets are a cheap way to help keep people healthy. The nets are treated with chemicals that prevent the bugs from biting people in their beds. Some health groups donate the nets to people in poor countries.

Bed nets help stop the spread of malaria. The nets protect sleeping people from mosquitoes that carry the disease.

In 2000, only about 2 percent of African children who lived in areas where malaria was a major problem slept under mosquito nets. By 2008, about 19 percent of African children had mosquito nets. Health organizations hope to continue improving that rate.

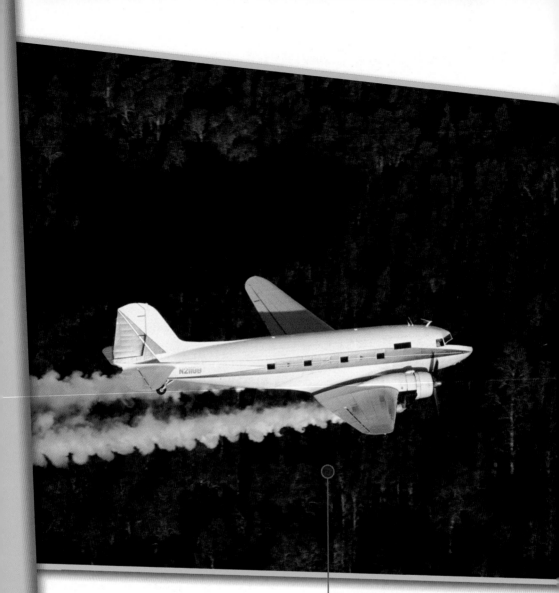

Spraying pesticide helps cut down on mosquitoes and other bugs.

MOSQUITOES ON THE MENU

Mosquitoes have many natural enemies. Many fish feed on mosquito eggs and larvae. A fish can eat 50 larvae in an hour. Bats, dragonflies, birds, and spiders also eat the bugs. Bats can eat 600 to 1,000 mosquitoes in an hour.

Nevertheless, the mosquitoes keep on coming! Governments and communities around the world wage a constant war against the insects. In many countries, including the United States, governments spray pesticides to reduce the mosquito population.

Don't Be Bug Bait!

Want to avoid being a snack for hungry mosquitoes? Here's the buzz on what to do.

- Wear long-sleeve shirts, long pants, and socks when you are near places where mosquitoes live.

- You can use an insect repellent to keep the bugs away. Follow the directions carefully. Have an adult apply the repellent.

- Plan your outdoor activities to limit outside time around dawn and dusk. At those times, mosquitoes are out in full force.

- Mosquitoes need water for breeding. Get rid of any standing water. Empty buckets, birdbaths, and other containers that might hold water.

- Be sure any torn screens are repaired. Keep the bugs outside!

- Use yellow lights instead of white lights outdoors. The white lights attract insects.

What should you do if you are bitten by a mosquito?

- Wash the bite with soap and water.

- Have an adult apply anti-itch cream or lotion.

- Don't scratch! Scratching can lead to infection.

- Placing an ice pack on the bite may help.

Avoid mosquito bites by taking simple precautions.

Chapter 6

Inside Job

So, you are not afraid of mosquitoes? You don't shudder at the thought of bedbugs or fleas? Try this fact on for size: Worms can live within your body and gnaw on your insides. Now, that's gross!

TALE OF THE TAPE

Tapeworms live in human intestines. The worms feed on digested food. They absorb the food's nutrients through their bodies. As they take in nutrients, the worms grow longer and longer.

Tapeworms are some of the largest human parasites. Just ask Sally Mae Wallace of Mississippi. She holds the world record for having the longest tapeworm—a 37-foot (11.2-m) monster!

Several types of tapeworms exist. They usually grow inside people who **ingest** water or undercooked meat that has tapeworm eggs. Doctors can treat the problem.

PINWORMS

Pinworms, or threadworms, also live inside people. Swallowing or inhaling pinworm eggs is the most common way of becoming infected. Pinworm eggs can spread through dust, clothing, bedding, or toys. Pinworms look like short strands of thread. They live in an infected person's **rectum**.

Strange but True

You have probably heard of Superman, Wonder Woman, and other fictional superheroes. Did you know you are pretty super yourself? All humans are superorganisms. We live with a huge number of microbes on us or in us. More than 500 different species of bacteria live in our bodies. It is lucky for us that most of these tiny creatures do not harm us. In fact, many microbes protect us from infections and illnesses!

This magnified tapeworm photo was colored green to show details clearly.

GOING BUGGY

Bugs are a fact of life. You can't live with them, and you can't live without them. Here are a few common bugs that can make life miserable.

Head louse

"Milhouse, we're living in the age of cooties," Bart Simpson warned his friend in an episode of *The Simpsons*. Bart was talking about lice. These vampire-like insects sip blood and make people itch and scratch.

Flea

A flea is an amazing bug. It can jump more than 200 times its own body length. To top that feat, a human would have to leap over the Empire State Building in New York City!

North American dust mite

These tiny bugs feed on flakes of dead skin cells. Nearly 100,000 dust mites can live on 11 square feet (1 square m) of carpet. Dust mites hide in sheets, on mattresses, and between floorboards. Sweet dreams!

Mosquito

There are about 2,700 species of mosquitoes throughout the world. Only the female bites. She can lay more than 200 eggs at a time. So when you swat one, there are always more!

Bedbug

Bedbugs like to snack on people. The bugs can hitch a ride in the luggage of travelers. They won't make you sick, but they will make you itch.

Pinworm

Pinworms, also known as threadworms, hang out in the lower intestine. Female worms often find their way "outside" at bedtime and leave eggs on pajamas and bedsheets.

The "Really Bad Bug" Award

Human botflies live in very warm, wet spots on Earth. These hairy creatures hook themselves onto skin and lay eggs there. After hatching, the larvae can burrow into the human brain!

Chapter 7

Battle of the Bugs

Who is winning the battle of the bugs? Scientists know of more than 1 million different kinds of bugs. Yet new bugs are discovered each year. Insects are moving into new areas, too. It's safe to say that the bugs outnumber us.

This stick insect is one BIG bug!

WARM-WEATHER FIENDS

Earth's temperature, on average, has been on the rise. **Global warming** has been blamed for many problems, such as melting sea ice and extreme weather. Many scientists say that long-term warming will also mean more insects than ever!

Why is it likely that higher temperatures will cause a boom in bugs? Warmth provides ideal conditions for many bug species to thrive. Most bugs have trouble surviving in low temperatures.

NEW BUGS ON THE BLOCK

Scientists are discovering new insects and related species all the time. The world's longest insect was recently found in Borneo. That is an island in Southeast Asia. The creature looks like a thin stick as long as a human arm! Even odder, the insect's eggs have wings. The eggs can drift on the wind. When it hatches, the new stick insect is already 2.5 inches (6.4 cm) long.

In 2002, scientists discovered a bug that belongs to a whole new order, or large category, of insects. Its nickname is "the gladiator." The creature is similar to both a grasshopper and a stick insect. Bug experts were excited about the find. No new order of insects had been discovered since 1915.

A warming Earth supports a growing insect population.

BUGS ON THE MOVE

As Earth warms, the number of disease-carrying insects is increasing. One bug that multiplies quickly is the yellow fever or dengue mosquito. As its name suggests, this species spreads the illnesses dengue fever and yellow fever. Scientists have now found this insect at high elevations in Central and South America. It had never before appeared at those elevations.

Other bugs are moving into new **habitats**, too. This change is happening around the world. The West Nile virus, for example, is infecting people in areas where it did not exist before. The microbe that causes cholera is spreading in warmer seas. Malaria has reached higher elevations in Africa.

Ants are moving to new areas as Earth warms.

Silkworms make silk.

WHAT DO YOU THINK?

What problems will arise as insects increase in number and invade new areas?

FRIENDS AND FOES

Ninety-seven percent of the world's bugs are our friends. The vast majority of these creatures are helpful to people. Silkworms, for example, provide us with silk. Honeybees make sweet, delicious honey for us to eat. Some insects **pollinate** plants. Dragonflies and spiders eat mosquitoes, gnats, flies, and other insects that bug us. Without these creatures, our lives would be very different.

An Increase by Degrees

Experts say that even a small rise in global temperature can start an explosion of Earth's insect population. Global warming increases the likelihood of wetter weather. Water is one of the main ingredients many insects search for when **breeding**.

SCIENCE AT WORK

ENTOMOLOGIST

Job Description: Entomologists study insects, including their origin, behavior, diseases, and life processes.

Job Outlook: Employment is expected to increase.
Earnings: $76,320 to $129,510, with a median income of $79,990

Source: Bureau of Labor Statistics

Conversation With an Entomologist

Glen Needham is an entomologist at Ohio State University in Columbus, Ohio. He specializes in the study of mites and ticks.

WHAT DOES AN ENTOMOLOGIST DO?

[I] investigate all kinds of things about "bugs"—how they live, and especially how to control the ones that are pests without harming the environment.

WHAT WAS YOUR TRAINING?

[I completed] my undergraduate training in biology at Southwestern Oklahoma State University. I had the chance to do research on tick physiology, earning my Ph.D. at Oklahoma State University.

HOW DID YOU GET INTERESTED IN BECOMING AN ENTOMOLOGIST?

Growing up in the Oklahoma Panhandle, there was not a lot to do indoors with only a black-and-white TV that gets one channel. I explored the outdoors, which included observing and sometimes collecting anything that moved, including spiders, insects, fish, birds, snakes, lizards, [etc.]. I would then return them to the wild.

WHAT DO YOU LIKE ABOUT THE WORK?

I like the freedom to do research on insects, mites, and ticks that impact public health. I love teaching about these fascinating organisms. We are currently studying a novel technology for controlling dust mites, bedbugs, and fleas using [a special kind of] light. If this pans out, we will be able to manage these pests without using chemicals.

FIND OUT MORE

BOOKS

Bailey, Jill. *Mosquito* (Bug Books). London: Heinemann, 2006.

Bueche, Shelley. *Parasites! Bedbugs.* Farmington Hills, MI: KidHaven Press, 2005.

DerKazarian, Susan. *You Have Head Lice!* (Rookie Read-About Health). San Francisco: Children's Press, 2005.

WEB SITES

Enchanted Learning: Mosquito
www.enchantedlearning.com/subjects/insects/mosquito/lifecycle.shtml
Find a printout that explains the mosquito life cycle.

Headlice.org
www.headlice.org/kids
This site offers a helpful guide to annoying head lice.

MSNBC
www.msnbc.msn.com/id/11916682
Read a *Dateline* report on bedbugs, and see the creatures up close!

GLOSSARY

abdomen: the rear part of an insect's body

allergy: troubling body reaction to material breathed in, touched, or eaten

antennae: pair of feelers on the head of an insect

antibiotics: a group of drugs that kills or inhibits the growth of bacteria

arachnids: animals, including spiders, mites, and ticks, that have bodies with two regions and eight legs

asthma: a chronic disease of the lungs

bacterium: a single-celled organism that lacks a nucleus. Some bacteria cause disease. (plural: **bacteria**)

breeding: producing offspring

bubonic plague: a serious disease caused by a bacterium

compound eyes: found in insects and some crustaceans, eyes made of many light-sensitive elements

cuticle: in invertebrates, a hard, protective outer covering

dander: scales from skin, hair, or feathers

ectoparasites: parasites that live outside the body of a host

endoparasites: parasites that live inside the body of a host

exoskeleton: a skeleton located on the outside of an animal; the hard covering of an animal's body

exterminators: people trained to kill pests

feces: animal waste matter

follicles: narrow openings in the skin from which hairs grow

global warming: an overall increase in Earth's average surface temperature

habitats: areas where specific species live and grow naturally

host: an animal that a parasite lives on or in

infestations: occasions of being overrun by parasites or pests

ingest: to take into the body

intestines: a long tube that extends down from the stomach and that carries and digests food

larva: a newly hatched form of an animal, such as an insect

mammals: warm-blooded animals that have a backbone, produce milk, and have hair or fur

mandibles: the paired mouthparts of an insect

microbes: an organism too small to be seen without a microscope

molt: to shed feathers or skin to make way for new growth

nymph: the form of an animal that is nearly adult

organisms: living creatures

parasites: animals that live in or on a host

pesticides: chemicals used to combat pests

pneumonic plague: a fatal form of the plague that attacks the lungs

pollinate: to transfer pollen, enabling plant reproduction

pores: tiny holes in the surface of the skin

prey: a creature caught or hunted for food

proboscis: a tube-like mouthpiece that insects use to suck in liquid food

rectum: a portion of the large intestine

repellent: something that drives an organism away

species: groups of plants or animals that are alike and can create offspring

stylet: a small, hollow, needle-like structure

thorax: the part of an insect's body between the head and the abdomen

INDEX

About the Author

John Perritano is an award-winning journalist who has written about science and the environment for various newspapers, magazines, and web sites. He is the author of many nonfiction titles for children. John holds a master's degree in U.S. history from Western Connecticut State University. John writes from Southbury, Connecticut, where he lives with his three dogs, three cats, and three frogs.